DANVILLE

This is a gift

*The Danville Library
Foundation*

CHIC
SIMPLE
®
Components

"I have a trunk
containing continents."

BERYL MARKHAM

CHIC
SIMPLE ®
Components

WITHDRAWN

P A C K I N G

ALFRED A. KNOPF   NEW YORK   1996

THIS IS A BORZOI BOOK
PUBLISHED BY ALFRED A. KNOPF, INC.

Copyright © 1994 by Chic Simple,
a partnership of
A Stonework, Ltd., and Kim Johnson Gross, Inc.

All rights reserved under
International and Pan-American Copyright Conventions.
Published in the United States by Alfred A. Knopf, Inc., New York,
and simultaneously in Canada by Random House of Canada Limited, Toronto.
Distributed by Random House, Inc., New York.

KIM JOHNSON GROSS   JEFF STONE

WRITTEN BY WALTER THOMAS
PHOTOGRAPHS BY JAMES WOJCIK
STYLED BY ANITA CALERO

DESIGN AND ART DIRECTION BY
THE VALENTINE GROUP
ILLUSTRATIONS BY GREGORY NEMEC
ICON ILLUSTRATION BY ERIC HANSON

Library of Congress Cataloging-in-Publication Data
Gross, Kim Johnson.
Chic Simple: Packing/Kim Johnson Gross, Jeff Stone, and Walter Thomas.
p. cm. – (Chic Simple)
ISBN 0-679-43219-1
1. Travel. 2. Luggage I. Gross, Kim Johnson. II. Stone, Jeff. III. Thomas, Walter.
G151.C47 1994
910'.2'02–dc20
94-4623
CIP

Manufactured in the United States of America
Published May 28, 1994
Second Printing, March 1996

CONTENTS

"The more you know, the less you need."

Chic Simple is a primer for living well but sensibly. It's for those who believe that quality of life comes not in accumulating things, but in paring down to the essentials. Chic Simple enables readers to bring value and style into their lives with economy and simplicity.

P A C K I N G

Packing is about choice. It's about confidence, knowledge, and purpose. It's about knowing the difference between what you want and what you need. It's just as much about who you are as where you're going. From which kinds of bag to take to what to put in them, the choice is yours. So whether you're travelling around the world or just going over to a friend's house for the night, knowing what to take with you is just as important as knowing what to do when you get there.

"Be sure to take a warm sweater!"

MOM

THE HISTORY OF PACKING

DATES TO WHEN MANKIND WAS RUDELY AWAKENED IN A CAVE BY THE RETURN OF ITS ORIGINAL OWNER. Packing became official with Herodotus the Greek, who's credited with being the First Tourist since he travelled only to satisfy his enormous curiosity. The first culture to produce tourism was

"Have a nice

Imperial Rome during *Pax Romana*. Wealthy Romans gathered up entire households: silken tents, bedding, commodes, cookware, gold platters, and crystal goblets. Armies further mastered the art—Napoleon insisted every soldier carry two pairs of boots in his knapsack. In America, carpetbaggers packed unscrupulously; in the West, cowboys packed pistols; and in outer space, astronauts packed Tang.

GREAT MOMENTS IN PACKING

Exiting from the Garden • Fanning out from the Cradle of Civilization •
Staying ahead of Alexander's army • Seafaring with the Vikings • Fleeing the
Plague • Riding with Die Walküre • Outracing the Oklahoma Sooners

GREAT TRAVEL BOOKS

The Odyssey, *Homer* • Narrow Journey to the Interior, *Basho* • The Can-
terbury Tales, *Geoffrey Chaucer* • The Razor's Edge, *Somerset Maugham* •
A Moveable Feast, *Ernest Hemingway* • On the Road, *Jack Kerouac* • Zen
and the Art of Motorcycle Maintenance, *Robert Persig*

trip, Dick."

BETTY FORD

BECAUSE IT'S THERE

The 1975 assault on the South-West face of Everest led by Chris Bonington
packed the following: 4 tons personal effects, 1 ton climbing equipment, 2 tons of
tentage, .75 tons cookware, 2 tons fuel, 1.5 tons oxygen, 13 tons food, 3 tons
general packing and plastic, and 1.5 tons of miscellaneous.

BECAUSE IT WAS THERE TOO

Thor Heyerdahl brought on his raft, Kon-Tiki, rations to last six men four
months: 56 cans of spring water, fruit, vegetables, and coconuts in large wicker
baskets, and eight wooden boxes—two for film, one per man for personal items.

Mobility.

We won't sit still. We want to move fast and take everything with us. To the office. To the gym. Away for the weekend. We're independence-minded but afraid of disconnection—from other people or from our work. From servants carrying libraries through jungles for explorer-scholars to jet-setting entrepreneurs whose only travel companion is a laptop computer, the need for a change of location has taken the constantly migrating human spirit to frontiers as exotic as the imagination and to destinations once as inconceivable as the moon. See you at the next stop, and keep in touch.

FOLD

Travel or campaign furniture was de rigueur for 19th-century colonialists. Expeditions didn't mean leaving luxury and convenience. Likewise the painters of the period whose search for the perfect light led them and their collapsible studios from Arles to Tahiti. The portable furniture they required became an art in itself.

UNFOLD

Louis Vuitton and Hermès continue the portable tradition, commissioning artists to produce exquisite, functional travel furniture.

How much to take. Travelling right doesn't always mean travelling light. Remember, there's no right or wrong to what to pack. Some people will only travel with what can comfortably fit into an over-the-shoulder bag. For others, nothing less than a set of matching suitcases will suffice. What you take depends more on who you are than where you're going. College student, business traveller, rock star, head of state, or family in transit, the only hard-and-fast rule is to take whatever it is you need to be yourself.

"Flying? I've been to almost as many places as my luggage!"

BOB HOPE

A GOOD IDEA

American Tourister's EasyTurn Pullman luggage was recognized by the ID Annual Design Review for being a "welcomed solution."

ABOUT WHEELS

Suitcase wheels are selling points for manufacturers and their quality and durability are as essential as any other part of the bag. Their ease of use is usually a matter of the distance between the handle and your hand, the remedy for which is a telescoping side handle.

A Room with a Point of View.

No matter where you're going, it's always nice to take a little something of yourself with you. That's why the Egyptian pharaohs filled their tombs with familiar objects like chairs, plates, and the family cat. Small children shouldn't travel without a comforting possession, a teddy or blanky. Similarly, you might find the going a little less disorienting if you take along something dear to you, a totem object, an irrational attachment, like the reading lamp that sits on your nightstand at home, favorite books and photographs, flowers and candles, a pillowcase or favorite throw, or even your spouse.

YOU ARE WHAT YOU TAKE

At least the Three Wise Men agree that what you pack can be the defining moment in your life.

"I never travel without my diary. One should always have something sensational to read in the train."

OSCAR WILDE

19

"Is that a gun in your pocket, or are you just happy to see me?"

MAE WEST

Simple Packing. The simplest piece of luggage is a pocket. It's extremely functional as well as occasionally fashionable. It is usually everyone's first understanding of the principles of packing. Marketers know its power and have created thousands of pocket-sized products— from pocket watches and pocketknives, to pocket New Testaments, and the Pocket Fisherman. And it is the type and number of pockets that mark the functionality of flight suits, fishing vests, overalls, and bush jackets.

POCKET NOTE

*The TR-63, Sony's first shirt-pocket model transistor radio,
circa 1957, was slightly larger than Japanese shirt pockets, so Sony issued
shirts with larger pockets to its salesmen, who could then demonstrate the
virtues of "pocketability" to interested customers.*

POCKET NOT

Never leave anything in the pockets of packed clothes.

FIFTH POCKET

*The mysterious pocket in a pocket on the right-hand side of Levi 501's was
originally for pocket watches; now useful for condoms.*

Making Checklists. Packing is about planning, and lists are essential to the planning process. First, compile a list of the minimum number of items you'll need regardless of your trip's duration or destination. Second, determine the best type of bag for the trip. Third, list items to take that are options to your basics. A list not only helps you to pack, but assists you when repacking, noting what's missing before leaving a hotel room. You might even want to consider attaching lists to bag tags so you'll know what's inside without opening them. Also when you come home from a trip, whether a river rafting adventure or three-day business trip, making a list of what worked can save time next time. Making lists may appear to be the preoccupation of compulsive personalities or NASA Mission Control experts, but packing for a trip is a difficult, confusing, and nearly always challenging exercise that can be tamed into an efficient operation by simply making lists.

[*A checklist for a* **DAY TRIP** *see page 81*]

"You can never be too paranoid."

C. E. CRIMMINS

DAY TRIPS

Every day is a day trip. You just don't always realize it because you keep travelling the same route. Remember how carefully you planned what to take to the office for your first day at the new job? But regardless of how unremarkable your daily journeys may eventually seem, packing properly for each one not only enhances the experience of each, but can make your life less subject to unpleasant surprises. The going can be made simpler, easier, and more manageable by learning how to prepare for each of your destinations.

"There is a time for departure even when there's no certain place to go."

TENNESSEE WILLIAMS

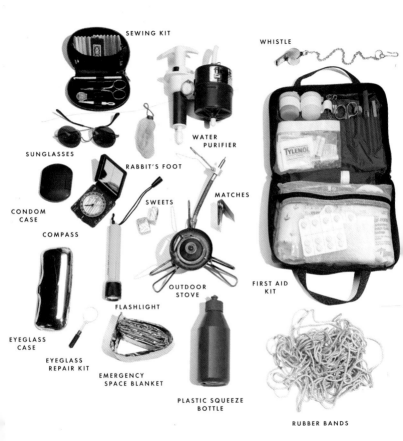

SEWING KIT

WHISTLE

WATER PURIFIER

SUNGLASSES

RABBIT'S FOOT

CONDOM CASE

COMPASS

SWEETS

MATCHES

TYLENOL

FIRST AID KIT

OUTDOOR STOVE

EYEGLASS CASE

FLASHLIGHT

EYEGLASS REPAIR KIT

EMERGENCY SPACE BLANKET

PLASTIC SQUEEZE BOTTLE

RUBBER BANDS

CANDLEHOLDER

HEADPHONES

FLASK

POCKET TISSUES

CLOTHESPIN

TOOTHBRUSH

SPOON

AQUA PILLTIMER

BATTERIES

Survival Gear. It's better to have it and not need it than to need it and not have it. If every walk were a space walk, you'd double-check your gear before stepping outside the door. Apply that logic to everyday life and you can rest easier, knowing that no matter what, you're prepared for it. Though maybe it's just easier to stay home and read Voltaire.

"Be prepared."

BOY SCOUT MOTTO

Tote Bags. People will tote anything—even a bale. And there is a tote for your every need. The most important feature is always its opening, which should be as large as possible, easy to access, and should zipper shut as an option. A wipe-clean, leak-proof liner for toting fresh vegetables or baby bottles is a detail worth the extra expense. Mesh pockets along the outside for bottles, baguettes, or a newspaper are handy. Choose a bag with zippered pockets both inside and out for securing necessities such as keys and money. And pay special attention to the straps; they should be long enough to allow the bag to hang comfortably from your shoulder.

MARKET BAGS
Going to market is a trip worthy of its own bag, and several types have been designed for the purpose. The simplest for everyday marketing is the string bag. It's a handy and ecological alternative to the paper or plastic sack the store will give you. String bags easily expand to accommodate surprisingly large loads, and fold nicely when empty to fit into a pocket or bag.

[*A checklist for* **A DAY TRIP** *see page 81*]

Choosing the right purse is as important as choosing the right outfit. When dressing up, the more elegant the outfit, the smaller the purse. A purse shouldn't be an inventory of your life and personality, so always strive to carry only what you absolutely need.

A Hierarchy of Bags.

Bags come in every conceivable size, shape, style, and material. Since the point of packing is organization, in order to efficiently carry everything you need, organize your belongings in a hierarchy of bags. Rather than simply finding a bag to put everything into, pack your bag with smaller bags, each serving a specific function—a makeup bag, a container for medicines, a coin purse, a pouch for pens and pencils. A color-coded system of pouches will allow you to locate your things even quicker. A bag hierarchy system also lets you easily transfer things between your briefcase, purse, gym bag, or suitcase.

[*A checklist for a* **HANDBAG** *see page 81*]

"The heaviest baggage
for a traveller is an
empty purse."

ENGLISH PROVERB

The Wallet.

Born in England as a watel or wattle, it was a bag for holding the necessities for a journey. Made of leather and open at the middle, it was the ancestor to both the knapsack and wallet. It has since downsized despite the ongoing importance of its contents—money, identification, phone, credit, and ATM cards. Although it's nice to be fat with cash, with wallets, thin is in. Whether carried in a purse, briefcase, back or breast pocket, it should be sleek and neat. Resist carrying more credit cards than you use, rotating them if you use several. Carry the amount of cash you wouldn't mind losing. And try to go easy on the family photographs.

HIP TIP

Don't keep a wallet in your back pocket during a long flight unless you're going to visit a long-lost chiropractor.

TRAVEL WALLETS

A quick remedy for different currencies is a specially designed travel wallet with various zippered compartments to isolate each currency.

[*A checklist for* **PACKING A WALLET** *see page 81*]

"The volume of paper expands to fill the available briefcases."

JERRY BROWN

Case Study. When it comes to business, your briefcase does your talking for you. If it's leather with locks it says, "Take me seriously. I'm the voice of authority!" If it's canvas or nylon it states, "I might be casual, but I'm still prepared." In terms of function, hardside cases can protect a portable phone, fax, and other electronic equipment, while softsided bags are lighter, more flexible in the volume they hold, and often can take more abuse and hard knocks.

GET A GRIP
To decide whether to select a briefcase with handles or a shoulder strap, consider the advantages of each: Some find carrying handle models more comfortable with the weight in hand while others prefer shoulder-strap styles that leave hands free.

THE RUCKSACK
In the '90s, the rucksack has gained ground on traditional briefcases. In business-speak, a rucksack proclaims, "Don't judge me, I'm my own person."

[*A checklist for* **A BUSINESS TRIP** *see page 81*]

35

The Mobile Workplace. There was a time when the pen and pad were the height of office technology, and one's importance was determined by the size of one's desk. Today, the office may still be a monkey on our back, but now it fits into a backpack. Digitalization is the ultimate concept in packing—it frees us from location. We can sit in a postcard setting while our thoughts travel at the speed of light along the information highway. We are conceptual commuters, nomads of the no-man's-land of cyberspace, wirelessly hooked up to remotely stationed hardware. Still, we're only as efficient as our batteries. And batteries are just one cost of the new mobility—all this convenience adds up not only in price but weight. Colin Fletcher, the famous backpacker, used to remove the paper handles on tea bags to save weight. This same attention pays off on the mobile office: buy light, it's worth it. Also don't forget to carry a power adapter with you on flights with layovers; a flight delay can exhaust batteries as well as patience.

"There's no there there."

GERTRUDE STEIN

TOOLS TO GO

Pager PIM *Cellular Phone* Laptop *Notebook* Electronic Agenda

Language Translator Currency Converter *Microrecorder* PDA *Batteries* Floppy carriers

Modem Modem Adapters *International Phone Plug Adapters*

NETWORKS

Internet *CompuServe* Applelink *America Online* Prodigy

"Beam me up, Scotty."

CAPTAIN KIRK

MODEM CONNECTION KIT

NEWTON PDA

POCKET PHONE
ORGANIZER

THREE-PRONG
ADAPTER

APPLE DUO LAPTOP

ZELCO CURRENCY
CONVERTER

ZELCO LIGHT

CELLULAR PHONE

PHONE ADAPTER
PLUG

NIKON LIGHT TOUCH

POST-IT POUCH

MICRORECORDER

ORGANIZER

THE MAGICAL MESSENGER BAG

Originally created for New York City bicycle messengers, a heavy-duty canvas carryall with a shoulder strap and Velcro® closure will prove wildly adaptable no matter what the weather or content needs. Washable, with a water-resistant lining, they come in a variety of sizes.

[*Checklists for* **INFANTS & TODDLERS** *and* **YOUNG CHILDREN** *see page 82*]

From Here to There. Choosing the right bag for commuting depends on the mode of transportation. Some types of commuting—by bike or on blades, or with an infant or children—are quite complicated. Fortunately, bags have been designed for nearly every occasion. Whatever the bag, it should have a compartment where the constant necessities of your daily commute—keys, tokens, stereo, paperback, employee I.D.—can be kept. Optimum mobility is linked to balance and a stable center of gravity, so select a bag that you can walk with easily, with shoulder straps as well as handles.

PETER FONDA ON
EASY RIDING

"Pack less, less than you'd ever imagine...there are always laundromats. First the things you don't need to get to right away: your clothes, bedroll, sleeping bag, and tent. On top of that, bungee your raingear and other things you need to get at quickly—like water and sunblock. I wear my leathers and recommend the kind that zip up over your jeans—you can take them off, put them under the bungee, and keep on trucking."

[*A checklist for* **A DAILY COMMUTE** *see page 82*]

The Wet/Dry Gym Bag.

Anyone who's serious about fitness will need a bag specifically designed for the purpose that's always packed and ready to go. The bag should be of light, durable nylon, and washable if possible. It should have a "wet" compartment for carrying damp towels and clothing, and a "dry" side for everything else. It should have a compartment for your sneakers, and a place for your toiletry bag. Outside pockets for newspapers or a water bottle and a secure inside pocket for delicate items like sports glasses and a personal stereo are features worth considering. If you skate or bike to the gym, choose a bag with shoulder straps.

TRAVELLING GYM
You should return from a trip looking better than when you left, and your workout schedule needn't be interrupted just because you travel. In fact, maintaining workout continuity is even more important on the road, when you're often subjected to jet lag, richer food, and longer work hours. A brief but intense exercise routine sweats out the day's stress and actually reduces fatigue.

[*A checklist for* **THE GYM** *see page 82*]

"Is forbidden to steal towels, please. If you are not
person to do such is please not read notice."

SIGN IN TOKYO HOTEL

Beachy Keen. Packing for the beach means dealing with three formidable forces—sun, surf, and sand. Although you might get by with nothing more than a baseball cap and a towel, a well-stocked bag is the best insurance against a beautiful day spoiled by hunger, a restless mind, and heat prostration. The best bag to pack is mesh—it's lightweight, sandproof, your things are visible, and wet towels and swim gear can dry quickly. A small, inner pouch is a handy feature for carrying your keys, money, and identification. Shoulder straps are nice in carrying the load through the dunes or down old beach stairs.

"The three most important things I take
on a long-distance yacht race are Labiosan lip
protector, sunglasses, and long underwear."

DENNIS CONNER

[*A checklist for* **THE BEACH** *see page 83*]

BAG OVERBOARD

For the rigors of aquatic adventures like waterskiing or kayaking, a water-resistant bag that floats can be life-preserving, at least for your things.

A Moveable Feast. Often a picnic is more than just lunch in the woods—it's a question of style. It could be a first step in a courtship and call for a fancy spread, or a trek through the wilderness requiring fancy footwork and the bare essentials. For the former, a wicker hamper is de rigueur, while for the latter we recommend a ripstop backpack. Just don't forget the bug spray.

A COOLER
BACKPACK
A functional innovation for day hikes, the backpack cooler has a zip-open lower "closed cell" foam-walled compartment that keeps food hot or cold, complete with a heat-sealed vinyl lining to prevent leaks.

"Reminds me of my safari in Africa…somebody forgot the corkscrew and for several days we had to live on nothing but food and water."

W. C. FIELDS

[*A checklist for* **THE PICNIC** *see page 83*]

EXPEDITIONS

The word expedition evokes images of Admiral Peary mushing to the North Pole or Neil Armstrong setting foot on the Sea of Tranquillity. But an expedition is any journey undertaken for a specific purpose, even when that purpose is to wander about purposelessly. In order to qualify as an expedition, however, your trip must be of a duration that requires you to pack a toothbrush. After that, what you take depends on who you are, where you're going, and the type of case you choose.

> "If you want to get away from it all
> don't take it all with you."
>
> THE FIRST RULE OF PACKING

The Overnight Bag. The shortest—and sometimes sweetest—trip of all is the overnighter. Packing for a sleep-over is like packing a carry-on for a longer journey, so the same rules apply for each. Remember, the need for utter practicality is greatest when travelling with only one bag. Assuming your trip is for fun and that business clothing isn't involved, the trick is to pack clothes that not only work well with each other, but that combine with what you'll wear to get there. Stick to basic colors—black, white, and gray or red—in fabrics that mix and layer nicely, like cotton, linen, and wool. Pack something that will also work in case you need to dress for dinner. Choose accessories for their ability to alter a look. Add a change of casual clothes, a good pair of loafers, and a swimsuit. Pack your clothing between sheets of tissue or plastic bags to prevent wrinkling. The travel kit goes on top. Don't forget your medicine. When in transit, wear your jewelry and blazer. Carry your raincoat or umbrella. Relax, you'll be home tomorrow.

[*A checklist for* **OVERNIGHT** *see page 83*]

"That night they took me out of the closet.
I would be transported in a garbage can—a brand-new,
thirty-gallon plastic container."

PATTY HEARST

STUFF SACKS

The stuff sack is an innovation that revolutionized backpacking. In a sport where packing is an art and utility a science, stuff sacks not only solve the problem of where things should go, but allow specific items to be located quickly and easily. When using stuff sacks, different color sacks can identify various contents—from hosiery to electronics. Mesh sacks are lightweight, see-through, and let water easily evaporate. A Ziploc bag also makes a great stuffer, especially for things that might leak, like nail polish. Moreover, the concept of the stuff sack is key to the successful packing of any type of bag.

The Carry-on. A carry-on bag is not only meant to be carried with you into the bus, train, or plane, but to be stowed there as well. Trying to stuff too many bags or too big a bag into an overhead bin is an avoidable hassle, so select one that meets the average allowable size for domestic airlines of 10" x 14" x 22". Carry-on bags run the price, style, and design gamut, so shop carefully—you will spend more time with it than with your travel partner. Among the newer innovations are wheeled versions with the telescoping handles, single-suit minigarment bags, and overnight "brief bags" with zippered expandable file folders for work papers.

MEDICINE KIT
Medicine is too important to be packed with checked luggage. Always keep your prescription drugs in your carry-on bag, preferably in their own case. Keep a printed list of all the drugs you're carrying, along with the name and telephone number of the prescribing physician so that you can reorder them easily and quickly.

[*A checklist for* **CARRY-ONS** *see page 83*]

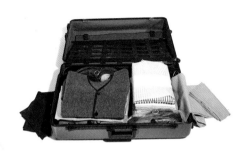

Wrinkle-Free Packing. This is the tissue, or plastic bag, method. This technique requires placing tissue paper between each layer of clothing, and there is a specific order that should be followed in packing. The tissue allows the garments to slide rather than settle or rub. First, interlock your belts and run them along the circumference of the suitcase. Next, place pants or trousers waistband to waistband with the legs left to hang outside of the case. Add tissue. Now, blouses or shirts, facedown and folded with a "long fold," turn-

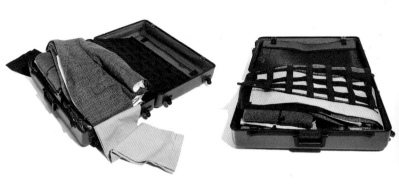

ing up the bottom of the garment a third to avoid a mid-belly crease. Tissue. Next, suit jackets and sports coats, turned inside out. Ties should be rolled up and placed in the jacket pockets. Another layer of tissue. Now take the pant legs and fold them over top. Tissue. A top layer of sweaters and socks, flat like you bought them, not rolled. Shoes—stuffed with underwear—along the sides in plastic grocery bags. Ditto toiletry kit. All else goes in another, smaller bag to be carried separately. Or better yet, left home on the bed and never missed.

Hard vs. Soft. When it comes to hard-sided or soft luggage, each has its merits. If wrinkle-free packing is your highest priority, choose hardsided. Softsided is lighter, stows more easily, and is gentler on the shins when wrestling it through an airport. Sudden impact, contact with sharp objects, and rain are the enemy. Soft survives drops off baggage carts best, but suffers punctures. Neither weathers a cloudburst well, though hard usually fares better. Hard breaks before it bends, so wheels, frames, and locks must be top quality. The weak point in soft luggage is usually the zippers and seam stitching so demand brass zippers and triple stitching.

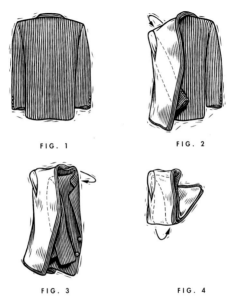

FIG. 1

FIG. 2

FIG. 3

FIG. 4

HOW TO PACK A JACKET

To begin with, empty all pockets. **1.** Holding the jacket facing you, place your hands inside the shoulders. **2.** Turn the left shoulder (but not the sleeve) inside out. **3.** Place the right shoulder inside the left shoulder. The lining is now facing out and the sleeves are inside the fold. **4.** Fold the jacket in half, put it inside a plastic bag, and place it in your bag.

HOW TO PACK PANTS

1. Check to make sure that all pockets are empty since keys or change may damage the fabric once the pants are packed. **2.** Pants should always be the first item packed, so place them onto the bottom of the bag with the waistband in the middle of the case, the legs actually falling outside the bag. (If you are packing two pairs, place them waistband to waistband, with the legs running in opposite directions.) **3.** Pack the rest of your things on top and then wrap the pants legs over the pile, placing one last remaining item over the legs to hold everything in place.

HOW TO PACK A SHIRT

1. Button all buttons, noting which front button falls below your waist. **2.** Lay the shirt face down on a flat surface and fold the sleeves back at the shoulder seam. **3.** Fold the tail up from the point of that button which is below your waistline. This will prevent the unpacked shirt from having a crease across your stomach. (Note: If you can plan ahead, have your shirts cleaned and folded at the laundry before your trip.)

HOW TO PACK SHOES

1. Shoes should always go in a bag—either cloth ones that can be cleaned, or disposable plastic bags from the grocery store. **2.** Place along the edge of a hard case to keep your folded clothes from shifting. In a duffel, shoes get packed first, at the bottom. **3.** Shoes can also carry socks, a coiled belt, extra eyeglasses, or overflow from your Dopp Kit, like a tube of sunscreen.

HOW TO PACK A TIE

1. Fold the tie in half. **2.** Place it on a sheet of tissue paper or length of plastic. **3.** Roll it up and put a loose rubber band around the coil. **4.** Place the rolled tie in the pocket of a jacket if you like.

[*A checklist for* **BASIC CLOTHES/WOMEN** *see page 83*]

Building a Travel Wardrobe.

The secret to successful packing is creating a complete system of dressing. Think in terms of putting together a collection of pieces in which color, fabric, and style work together. Pick classic silhouettes, and stick to neutrals with one additional color. (Black is always in fashion, goes anywhere, and doesn't show dirt.) Versatility is key, so choose clothes that move easily from day to dinner—a big white shirt, a little black dress, a good walking heel. Basics can be dressed up with the right accessories, like a generous scarf. And don't overlook the obvious—leggings, bodysuits, and a sarong.

VERSATILITY

Items that perform double duty should be taken twice as seriously. A poncho that turns into a tent, a silk scarf that transforms into a skirt, a T-shirt that serves as a nightshirt, or a pair of thick socks that work as a camera case and personal stereo cover.

A WRINKLE IN TIME

When shopping for a travel wardrobe, choose clothes that resist wrinkles. A good way to test is to grab the cloth, crush it up in your fist for 30 seconds, then let go. The degree to which the fabric wrinkles will give you a good idea as to how it will react after several hours in a suitcase.

Versatility and comfort should describe your travel wardrobe. Choose a dozen classic items—from blue jeans to a navy blazer—then put them together in your own way. The rest of the trip will take care of itself.

"A vacation is where you take twice the clothes
and half the money you need."

ANONYMOUS

[*A checklist for* **BASIC CLOTHES/MEN** *see page 84*]

It's All in the Mix. Clothes should mix to match your activities, so combine functional outdoor or street-smart styles with your business clothing. Keep in mind that solid colors mix best—navy, gray, or black and white, plus one color. Keep it simple in the shirt and tie departments, packing only colors and patterns versatile enough to mix with everything. Choose a sports coat that can be worn for business as well as casual. A pair of gray flannel dress trousers will see you through any occasion. When in transit, carry, don't pack, your overcoat. And never wear your suit on the plane unless you're going right into a business meeting.

BASIC BLACK (AND WHITE)

If you can only take one tie with you, make it a classic black knit. It goes with everything, and is as dressy or casual as whatever you wear it with. It's nearly impossible to wrinkle, and won't show stains. Another indispensable travel companion is a simple white cotton button-down shirt. Worn with jeans or a suit, there isn't anywhere where it won't be just right.

When choosing what to pack, consider all the options, but exercise some logic. Keep it simple. Easy does it. Navy is natty. Plain is elegant. White goes with everything. Stay relaxed. Don't be afraid to wear the same thing twice.

"One should bring a grey suit, not too formal for
impromptu gatherings, but if the need arises it is
dressed down enough for a funeral."

THE ACCIDENTAL TOURIST

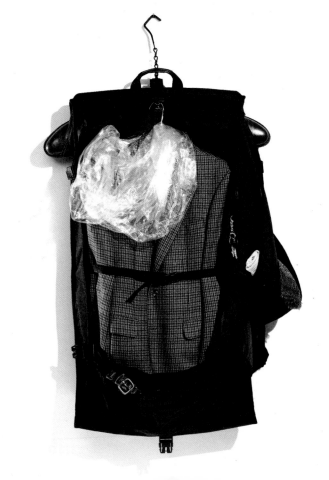

Garment Bags. The idea behind garment bags is that your clothing hangs in the bag exactly as in your closet. Some manufacturers refer to their garment bags as "walk-in closets," although the average design is a three-to-five suiter. Most come with several zippered compartments, usually designed to perform a specific function—carry shoes, folded shirts, or toiletries. A bag with mesh compartments lets you find things without unpacking. Smaller is better, a lesson learned after filling one up and not being able to lift it. The best bags are known as "bend over backwards" bags because of the direction they close, which helps prevent wrinkling.

TWO TIPS

Pack your clothes right from the dry cleaners. The plastic covers let them slide over each other, reducing wrinkling. Avoid bags that don't let you use regular hangers so you don't have to worry about lost or damaged hangers.

FEAR OF FLYING

Avoid checking a garment bag if possible—baggage handlers detest them because they're usually too fat to hang, too heavy to lift, and the hooks can be lethal.

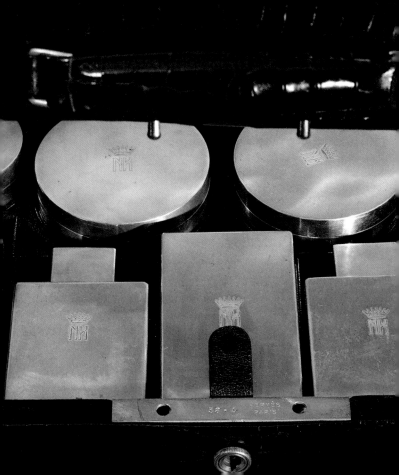

THE VANITY OF VANITIES

*Like the luxury ocean liners, mahogany-paneled passenger trains, and prop
engine airplanes of yesteryear, rich-girl vanity cases have become museum pieces.
Today's cosmetic case may very well be the Ziploc bag.
Clean, light, and transparent, its utility and simplicity are
a perfect example of form and function.*

Travel Kits. Toiletry bags are to travel what medicine cabinets are to bathrooms. Yet despite being so vital, travel kits are often treated as an afterthought. It should be durable and big enough to hold the basics, yet small enough to pack into another bag. It should be water-resistant, spill-proof, and stain-resistant. Insist on a wide mouth with a strong zip closure, at least one interior pocket, and if you don't want to share your prescription drugs, it should lock. A hanging kit with see-through mesh compartments will give you the easiest access, allow wet items to dry, and let you keep your toiletries packed for quick getaways.

DOPP STORY

Men's travel kits are often referred to as Dopp Kits. The term comes from a Chicago leather goods manufacturer called Dopp, who successfully marketed the bags.

SIZE MATTERS

If you're going on a short trip, don't pack big bottles of shampoo and conditioner. Either get a set of small plastic bottles with screw tops and only take what you need, or go to a pharmacy that sells products in travel sizes.

[*A checklist for a* **TRAVEL KIT** *see page 84*]

Plugging In and Turning On.

Although any decent hotel has a wake-up service, and it's not uncommon to find rooms equipped with a hair dryer, the most reliable way to travel is with a healthy sense of skepticism. Always rely on yourself and good quality hardware. When selecting a hair dryer or steamer, shop around for the most compact models that don't sacrifice important features. A travel alarm should have a luminescent face, and you might consider one that displays two time zones. Most countries use 220 volts, so buy a set of electrical adapters, since the number and size of prongs needed for electrical outlets varies. Throw out the case they come in and use a stuff sack.

The Duffel. Known as a "tube trunk," the duffel is the most basic, no-frills carryall ever devised. It packs quickly and absorbs abuse without complaint. Pick a duffel that's big enough to get the job done but small enough to drag through an airport. Get a padded shoulder strap, but remember that straps and buckles tend to get hung up in baggage conveyors. The beefier and heavier the fabric the better. Heavy-duty canvas is great, but 12-ounce Cordura nylon or 16-ounce ballistic nylon is slashproof and will endure anything. Get triple stitching, taped seams, a water-resistant vinyl liner, a #10 zipper in solid brass, and a foam-padded bottom.

When packing a duffel, put shoes in first, at the bottom, along with the things you need the least. Roll cottons and knits, including underwear, sweaters, and pants, and pack them as bumpers against each other. Place the rolls either upright or on their sides, whichever fits best. When packing delicate or semidelicate items, use tissue paper or plastic dry cleaner bags to protect them and prevent wrinkling. Place toiletries in Ziploc bags and bury them between garments. Finally, shore up the sides with hard items, like books and an umbrella.

"Lots of parents pack off their troubles and send them to summer camp."

RAYMOND DUNCAN

The Checklists. Only Noah had a definitive list, but we have created basic lists for different situations to use as a starting point for your own travel plans. Copy and create your own list to suit your situation. Place the list in a safe place such as a filofax or wallet for easy access and quick reference and update it after the trip.

REASONS FOR MAKING A PACKING LIST

1. To simplify and organize the packing process
2. To control the number of items packed
3. To prevent the omission of vital items
4. To guard against over-packing
5. To help clarify clothing options and combinations
6. To assist with claims against lost luggage

BEFORE YOU LEAVE HOME

1. Arrange to have your mail held at the post office or collected by a friend
2. Stop all deliveries to your home
3. Arrange for your pets, plants, and lawn
4. Notify neighbors of your absence and how to reach you
5. Leave a house key with a friend
6. Reconfirm your airline ticket and other reservations
7. Set timers or leave lights on
8. Empty refrigerator and turn it on low
9. Turn off hot water
10. Lock all doors, windows, and car

THE TEN ESSENTIALS

The Mountaineers, founded in 1906, is a non-profit outdoor activity and conservation club, based in Seattle, Washington. They established a list of Ten Essentials that should always be taken on any outing, whether for an hour ramble or an expedition.

1. Flashlight with an extra bulb and batteries
2. Map
3. Compass
4. Extra food
5. Extra clothing
6. Sunglasses
7. First aid
8. Pocketknife
9. Matches and waterproof container
10. Firestarter-candle

DAY TRIP
from page 22

_ Address book
_ Briefcase
_ Driver's license/identification
_ Eyeglasses – regular/sun
_ Hairbrush/comb
_ Handbag
_ Handkerchief
_ Itinerary confirmation
_ Keys – car, home, office
_ Medicines
_ Money items
_ Pens/pencils
_ Reading materials
_ Safety pins
_ Sewing kit
_ Tickets
_ Tissues

HANDBAG
from page 30

In addition to Day Trip Checklist, consider bringing:
_ Cosmetics (lipstick, compact)
_ Emery board
_ Perfume
_ Tampons

PACKING A WALLET
from page 33

_ Auto club membership card
_ Billfold
_ Business cards
_ Cash
_ Checkbook
_ Credit cards
_ Driver's license
_ Family pictures/ photographs
_ Health insurance card
_ Telephone card
_ Traveller's checks

BUSINESS TRIP
from page 35

_ Address book
_ Advertising materials
_ Airline tickets
_ Appointment book
_ Briefcase
_ Business cards
_ Calculator
_ Computer – accessories
_ Confirmations – hotel, etc.
_ Correspondence
_ Credit cards
_ Expense forms
_ Files
_ Highlighters
_ Letters of credit
_ Markers

_ Meeting materials
_ Money
_ Notebooks
_ Paper clips
_ Passport
_ Pencils/pens
_ Portfolio
_ Presentation materials
_ Price lists
_ Proposals
_ Publications
_ Purchase order forms
_ Reports
_ Rubber bands
_ Samples
_ Stamps
_ Stapler, staples
_ Stationery, envelopes
_ Tape recorder/tapes
_ Time records
_ Work pads

"Bring everything, and have someone else carry it."

FRAN LEBOWITZ

INFANTS & TODDLERS
from page 40

_ Baby pillow
_ Bibs
_ Blankets
_ Bottles/nipples/caps
_ Burping towels
_ Crib bumpers
_ Disposable bags
_ Disposable diapers
_ Eating utensils
_ Formula/milk
_ Jacket/coat
_ Juices
_ Lotions/ointments
_ Lovey
_ Medication
_ Music tapes
_ Pacifier
_ Paper towels
_ Port-a-crib
_ Tape player
_ Teething biscuits
_ Thermometer
_ Toy
_ Training cup
_ Vitamins
_ Washcloths/wipes
_ Waterproof changing
   sheet

> "When I was
> a kid my
> parents
> moved a lot—
> but I always
> found them."
>
> R O D N E Y
> D A N G E R F I E L D

YOUNG CHILDREN
from page 40

_ Address book with
   important phone
   numbers
_ Books/magazines
_ Crayons/pencils
_ Electronic games
_ Games
_ Gum (for airline travel)
_ Identification
_ Juice packs
_ Medicine
_ Money
_ Name tags with
   destination—for child
   & luggage
_ Paper
_ Snack food

_ Spare batteries
_ Toys/cards

A DAILY COMMUTE
from page 41

_ Auto club membership
_ Cellular phone
_ Coins/tokens
_ Dictaphone
_ Driver's license
_ Driving shoes
_ Eyeglasses – regular/sun
_ First aid kit
_ Gas credit cards
_ Keys
_ Maps
_ Music
_ Notepad
_ Pen/pencils
_ Tissues
_ Water

THE GYM
from page 42

_ Athletic supporters
_ Headbands/elastic bands
_ Membership card
_ Padlock for locker
_ Plastic bag for wet
   things
_ Shirts
_ Shorts
_ Sneakers

_ Socks
_ Sport bras
_ Stretch-wrap bandages
_ Towels
_ Warm-up suit
_ Wristbands

THE BEACH
from page 44

_ Bathing suit
_ Beach blanket
_ Beach toys
_ Cover-up
_ Flip-flops
_ Folding chair
_ Food and drinks/water
_ Goggles
_ Hat with visor
_ Ice pack
_ Lip balm
_ Nose plugs
_ Pail and shovel
_ Plastic bag for wet suit
_ Reading material
_ Sunblock
_ Sunglasses
_ Swim fins
_ Towels
_ Umbrella

THE PICNIC
from page 47

_ Blanket/ground sheet
_ Cups

_ Folding chairs
_ Food and beverages
_ Garbage bag
_ Icebox/pack
_ Insect repellent
_ Matches
_ Moist towelettes
_ Plastic/paper bags
_ Plates
_ Radio
_ Straws
_ Sunblock
_ Swiss Army knife
_ Thermos
_ Umbrella
_ Utensils

OVERNIGHT
from page 51

_ Dopp Kit
_ Nightclothes
_ Shirt
_ Socks/stockings
_ Underwear

CARRY-ON
from page 55

_ Address book
_ Camera and film
_ Car/house keys
_ Confirmations
_ Electronic equipment
_ Eyeglasses – regular/sun

_ Foreign language
    dictionary
_ Handbag
_ Identification
_ Jewelry
_ Medicine
_ Money
_ Outerwear
_ Passport/visas
_ Portable CD player
_ Reading material
_ Ticket
_ Toothbrush/-paste
_ Water

BASIC CLOTHES/WOMEN
from page 62

_ Belt
_ Black dress
_ Black shoes
_ Bodysuit and leggings
_ Handbag
_ Hosiery and underwear
_ Jeans
_ Jewelry
_ Raincoat
_ Scarf
_ Shorts
_ Sleepwear
_ Sneakers
_ Sports clothes
_ Suit with pants and skirt
_ Sweater
_ Swimsuit and sarong

- T-shirt
- Vest
- Walking shoes
- Watch
- White shirt

BASIC CLOTHES/MEN
from page 66

- Athletic shoes
- Belt
- Black knit tie
- Black or brown shoes
- Business suit
- Dress shirts (two white, three solid colors)
- Jean or sports shirt
- Jeans
- Khaki or corduroy pants
- Navy blazer
- Sleepwear
- Socks and underwear
- Sports clothes
- Swimsuit
- Trench coat
- Vest
- Watch
- White T-shirt

TRAVEL KIT/MALE
from page 75

- Adapter kit
- Aftershave lotion
- Baggies for spillables
- Body lotion

- Cleanser
- Cologne
- Condoms
- Cotton sticks
- Dental floss
- Dentures/case/cleaner
- Deodorant
- Foot powder
- Hair care
  - Coloring
  - Comb
  - Dryer
- Lip balm
- Moisturizer
- Mouthwash
- Nail clippers
- Razor/blades
- Shampoo/conditioner
- Shaving cream
- Soap
- Soap box
- Styptic pencil
- Sunscreen
- Swiss Army knife
- Tissues
- Toothbrush
- Toothpaste
- Tweezers

TRAVEL KIT/FEMALE
from page 75

- Baggies for spillables
- Bath oil
- Birth control

- Body lotion
- Cleanser
- Compact
- Cosmetic kit
  - Blush
  - Concealer
  - Eye pencil
  - Eye shadow
  - Eyelash curler
  - Eyeliner
  - Face powder
  - Foundation
  - Lip balm
  - Lip liner
  - Lipstick
  - Mascara
  - Nail polish
- Cotton balls
- Cotton sticks
- Dental floss
- Dentures/case/cleaner
- Deodorant
- Douche bag/lotion
- Emery boards
- Eye cream
- Eye makeup remover
- Foot powder
- Hair care
  - Bobby pins
  - Clips
  - Comb
  - Curlers
  - Curling iron
  - Dryer

- Rubber bands
- Scrunchies
- Spray
_ Hand lotion
_ Makeup remover
_ Moisturizer
_ Mouthwash
_ Nail polish remover pads
_ Night cream
_ Perfume
_ Razor/blades
_ Sanitary products
_ Sewing kit
_ Shampoo/conditioner
_ Shower cap
_ Soap
_ Soap box
_ Sunscreen
_ Swiss Army knife
_ Tampons
_ Tissues
_ Toothbrush
_ Toothbrush holder
_ Toothpaste
_ Tweezers

MEDICINE CHECKLIST

_ Antiseptic lotion
_ Aspirin
_ Band-aids
_ Cold remedies
_ Diarrhea medication
_ Emergency contacts
_ Identification bracelet

_ Insect repellent
_ Medical information –
  allergies, medications,
  and blood type
_ Moleskin for blisters
_ Physician's name,
  address, and telephone
_ Prescription medications
_ Sunblock
_ Thermometer
_ Throat lozenges
_ Vitamins

INTERNATIONAL CHECKLIST

_ Addresses for
  correspondence
_ Auto registration
  (if driving)
_ Cash, including some in
  the currency of the
  country to which you are
  travelling
_ Credit cards
_ Emergency contacts
_ Extra prescription glasses
  and contacts
_ Insurance papers
_ International driver's
  license
_ Lightweight tote bag for
  purchases
_ Medical information
_ Passport, visas, health
  certificates

_ Phrase book or
  dictionary
_ Special prescriptions and
  medications
_ Sunglasses
_ Tickets and travel
  documents
_ Travel itinerary
_ Traveller's checks and
  personal checks

A CHECKLIST FOR A PET

_ Blanket
_ First aid kit
_ Flea collar
_ Food
_ Grooming tools
_ Leash and muzzle
_ Name and address tag
_ Pet carrier
_ Pet toys
_ Plastic bowls
_ Proof of immunizations
_ Veterinarian certificate
  of good health
_ Water

"From the cradle
to the coffin
underwear comes
first."

BERTOLT
BRECHT

first aid.

If something can go wrong it probably will—but not until you're on the road. Prepare for disaster, and if it strikes, at least you'll be able to say you did all you could before the last minute. Information is often the best weapon for coping with difficult situations. But no matter what, your most indispensable travel item is a heavy-duty sense of humor.

FLYING

JET LAG HELP
For about $10, California-based TimeZone Management Consulting will create a timetable customized to your trip to beat travel fatigue, including optimal flights, in-flight meals, sleep recommendations, and sunlight schedules for the day after arrival. 714/552-4660.

THE LIMITS OF LUGGAGE
Although the FAA allows each airline to determine for themselves the dimensions for carry-on luggage and the number of pieces one can carry on board, federal guidelines recommend a limit of two pieces, including a briefcase.

Bags stowed under a seat can only measure 9" x 14" x 22". For bags stored overhead, the limit is 10" x 14" x 36". Garment bags should measure no more than 4" x 23" x 45".

MEMORY LOSS
When checking a computer through airport security, always send it with your carry-on luggage through the X-ray machine, which won't damage your equipment in any way. Taking it through the magnetically charged metal detector, however, can cause the contents of your computer's hard drive to be erased.

"Whenever I travel I like to keep the seat next to me empty. I found a great way to do it. When someone walks down the aisle and says to you, 'Is someone sitting there?' just say, 'No one—except the Lord.'"

CAROL LEIFER

HEALTH

TIME TO TAKE YOUR MEDICINE
Palm-sized to fit in your pocket, purse, or carry-on, the Aqua Pilltimer by Zelco holds your prescription drugs, and features an easy-to-set alarm for timely dispensation. For easy ingestion, it has a 2-ounce water reservoir with built-in straw. About $25. 800/431-2486.

LOWER-TRACT TREAT
When visiting a country whose cuisine is new to you, eat a healthy serving of locally produced yogurt as soon as possible. Its live but benign bacterial culture should soften any culinary shocks.

HOW TO FIND A DOCTOR
The International Association for Medical Assistance to Travelers (IAMAT) is a voluntary organization of hospitals, health care centers, and more than 3,000 English-speaking, Western-trained doctors practicing in over 140 countries. All participants adhere to a standard scale of fees. Call 716/754-4883 for their free directory.

THE FAX OF LIFE
If you end up in an emergency room, you don't want hospital staffers wondering how to track down your family or doctor. A $20-a-year membership with LifeFax allows a physician to call a toll-free number and have your vital medical information faxed to him within minutes. 800/487-0329.

GYM DANDY
Although more and more hotels are offering health clubs for guests, you're still better off packing your own. No larger than a shaving kit when folded, among the most versatile and travel-friendly are systems based on continuous resistance, in which the bulk of the machine is comprised of surgical tubing. An exercise tool used for years by professional sports teams like the San Francisco Giants and Chicago Cubs, rubber tubing is great for strength training, allows one to work specific muscles effectively, and can be adjusted for any level of difficulty.

LANGUAGE

SIGN LANGUAGE
Why speak loudly or play charades with people whose language you don't speak? For $5 you can get Quickpoint, a laminated card printed with 390 pictorial symbols, from a telephone to a salt shaker with the international "no" symbol stamped on over it. Gaia Publications, Box 239, Alexandria, VA; 703/548-8794.

CLOTHES

WRINKLE REMOVER
The movement and shifting of your packed clothing is the major cause of wrinkling. Fill empty spaces in your suitcase or bag with rolled-up socks, T-shirts, underwear or wads of tissue or crumpled plastic dry cleaner or grocery bags.

LAUNDRY IN THE HOTEL ROOM
Most hotels can do laundry in a matter of hours, but the charges can leave you feeling wrung out. Hanging especially wrinkled clothing in a bathroom made steamy by letting the hot water in the shower run should do the trick. Socks and underwear can be cleaned in your bathroom sink, using shampoo—just rinse well.

LUGGAGE

LUGGAGE HOSPITALS
Wherever there's a big airport, there's a luggage repair shop nearby. Many airlines have authorized repair companies in each city they service, and they're usually listed in the Yellow Pages. Locks, handles, straps, wheels, and zippers can usually be repaired quickly the same day. Holes can be patched, slashes sewn, and corners reinforced.

AN EXCELLENT I.D.
If your luggage looks like a lot of other people's, put an unusual or brightly colored tag or marker on it. Also, since tags of any type fall off, paste a label with your name and address inside your bag as well.

GENERAL INFORMATION

TRAVEL-CHALLENGED
Society for the Advancement of Travel for the Handicapped (SATH), 718/858-5483. Also, the Disabled Traveler's Friendship Network (DTFN) can be contacted through Compuserve for information and advice. 72066,212 comp.

POLITICAL ALERT
State Department warnings and detailed information concerning the political conditions of 196 countries may be obtained by fax or ordered over the phone and sent by mail. Likewise, visa information on any country you might wish to visit. Telephone: 202/647-5225; fax: 202/647-3000; modem: 202/647-9225.

> "It goes without saying that you should never have more children than you have car windows."

ERMA BOMBECK

COSMETICS INDUSTRY
To keep cosmetics from melting when travelling keep the following in mind: Refrigerate them in the summer months so that they're not already soft before you head out. Never leave them in a glove compartment or locker. When picnicking in the sun, place them in the cooler along with your drinks. On the Rocks, of Millennium Beverly Hills, makes an insulating bag especially for keeping your cosmetics cool: 800/795-2405.

DON'T SING THE BLUES
Sew a steel guitar string into the strap of your neck pouch—it will foil the thief who tries to cut the strap (from Eastern Mountain Sports's booklet, Travel Safety & Health Tips).

HIP REPLACEMENT
The real drag of a lost or stolen wallet usually comes from the hassles associated with replacing your identification and credit cards. Take a minute and photocopy the contents of your wallet.

FAX ATTACK
If you intend to fax from your laptop while overseas, you'll also need a phone plug adapter. Some kits include two, one for Europe and another for Japan, but in some cases you'll actually need to use a set of alligator clips to attach your plug to the phone wires. Consult your computer manufacturer or place an inquiry with the Internet.

LIGHTEN UP
Most hotel rooms are underlit by household standards, so take along a few 75- or 100-watt lightbulbs for reading and desk work.

LAST ITEMS

Pack your small camera, film, personal stereo, or travel alarm into shoes for protection.

Always take more socks and underwear than you think you'll need.

Pack more pants than sports coats.

Either leave space for return items or pack a collapsible case.

It's very hard to tell if a checked shirt is wrinkled.

Khaki pants and black jeans will save you over and over.

The best way to pack less is to buy a smaller suitcase.

You should be able to carry your bag at least half a mile.

A photocopy of your birth certificate can expedite the replacement of a lost or stolen passport.

PACKING CHART

To determine the minimum amount of clothes needed for the maximum amount of activities
on a given trip, a packing chart can serve as an effective visual aid.

- First, map out the days you will be travelling in a vertical column. Then make three adjacent columns, to designate what to wear in the A.M. and P.M. each day and a column for extras.

- In the extras column, note the clothing and equipment you will need for special activities like tennis or formal wear, and list other basic items like nightwear, underwear, an umbrella, etc.

- In the A.M. column, designate the first day and last day as travel days. Choose clothes that are comfortable and versatile enough to be worn during your trip. Record in appropriate slots.

- Next, determine the type of clothes you will need for your trip. Try to limit yourself to a neutral color scheme that can be accented with colorful accessories.

- Then choose one wardrobe basic, perhaps a suit, that can achieve different looks with accessories. Determine the days and nights it can be worn. Record in appropriate slots.

- If needed, choose a second wardrobe basic. Try to fill in the remaining slots.

- Next choose accessories: shirts, sweaters, ties or jewelry, scarves or vests that will complement each wardrobe basic and help to create a variety of looks.

- At this point, it should be easy to determine if an extra garment is needed to complete your travel wardrobe needs.

- Now look at the chart and decide on shoes—they're bulky and heavy, so choose wisely.

- Pack this chart in your bag. It will remind you of your wardrobe scheme, and help you recognize the unnecessary and the essential.

	A.M.	P.M.	EXTRAS
MONDAY – *travel day*			
TUESDAY			
WEDNESDAY			
THURSDAY			
FRIDAY			
SATURDAY			
SUNDAY – *travel day*			

where.

A Chic Simple store looks out on the world beyond its shopwindow. Items are practical and comfortable and will work with pieces bought elsewhere. The store can be a cottage industry or a global chain, but even with an international vision it is still rooted in tradition, quality, and value.

FREEDOM OF CHOICE

Even as the world shrinks and chain stores expand globally, there are plenty of locales where choice is limited if there is any choice at all. However, most manufacturers today can aid you in finding a store or even mail direct to you. The U.S. numbers listed below will help give you freedom of choice.

American Tourister	800/635-5505
Boyt Luggage	800/366-2698
Coach	800/223-8647
Delsey	800/558-3344
Ghurka	800/243-4368
Hartmann Luggage	800/331-0613
Hermès	800/441-4488
Lark	800/421-LARK
Louis Vuitton	800/285-2255
Patagonia	800/638-6464
Polo/Ralph Lauren	800/653-7656
REI (Recreational Equipment Inc.)	800/426-4840
Tumi Luggage	800/322-8864
Zelco Industries	800/431-2486

United States

ALABAMA

PARISIAN
2100 River Chase Galleria
Birmingham, AL 35244
205/987-4200 or
205/940-4000 for U.S. listings
*(Leather goods and travel
accessories)*

CALIFORNIA

THE AUTHENTIC
TRAVELLER
9240 Jordan Avenue
Dept. NR3
Chatsworth, CA 91311
800/826-7221 or
818/407-9500
(Classic travelers' vests)

FRED SEGAL
8100 Melrose Avenue
Los Angeles, CA 90046
213/651-3342
(Luggage and accessories)

GEORGIA

RICH'S
Lenox Square Shopping Mall
3393 Peachtree Road, NE
Atlanta, GA 30326
404/231-2611
(Department store)

ILLINOIS

MARSHALL FIELDS
111 North State Street
Chicago, IL 60602
312/781-1000

IOWA

BOYT LUGGAGE
509 Hamilton Avenue
Iowa Falls, IA 50126
800/366-2698 or
515/648-4626

LANDMARK LUGGAGE
& GIFTS, INC.
2165 NE 108th Street,
Suite E
Des Moines, IA 50325
515/278-2004
(Luggage and sports gear)

MAINE

L. L. BEAN FACTORY
OUTLET
151 High Street
Ellsworth, ME 04605
207/667-7753
(Duffel bags)

MASSACHUSETTS

LOUIS, BOSTON
234 Berkeley Street
Boston, MA 02116
617/262-6100

MONTANA

DANA DESIGN
333 Simmental Way
Bozeman, MT 59715
406/587-4188
(Backpacks)

NEW JERSEY

TUMI LUGGAGE
250 Lackland Drive,
Suite 11
Middlesex, NJ 08846
800/322-8864 or
908/271-9500
(Backpacks)

NEW YORK

New York City

AD HOC SOFTWARES
410 West Broadway
New York, NY 10012
212/925-2652
(Travel gear)

ASPREY
725 Fifth Avenue
New York, NY 10022
212/688-1811
(Luggage and accessories)

BETTINGERS
80 Rivington Street
New York, NY 10002
212/475-1690

BOTTEGA VENETA
635 Madison Avenue
New York, NY 10022
800/662-5020 or
212/371-5511
(Luggage and handbags)

CROUCH &
FITZGERALD
400 Madison Avenue
New York, NY 10017
212/755-5888
(Fine luggage and accessories)

E. VINCENT LUGGAGE
1420 Sixth Avenue
New York, NY 10019
212/752-8251

FLORIS
703 Madison Avenue
New York, NY 10021
212/935-9100
(Travel gear)

GHURKA
41 East 57th Street
New York, NY 10022
212/826-8300
(Luggage and travel gear)

GOLDPFEIL
777 Madison Avenue
New York, NY 10021
212/472-4500
(Luggage and travel gear)

GUCCI
685 Fifth Avenue
New York, NY 10022
212/826-2600
(Purses, handbags, and luggage)

HERMÈS
11 East 57th Street
New York, NY 10022
212/751-3181
(Fine luggage, handbags, and accessories)

INNOVATION LUGGAGE
200 World Trade Center,
Concourse Level
New York, NY 10048
212/432-1090

LOUIS VUITTON
49 East 57th Street
New York, NY 10022
212/371-6111
(Leather luggage and accessories)

MCM
57 East 57th Street
New York, NY 10022
212/688-2133

PARAGON
867 Broadway
New York, NY 10011
212/255-8036
(Duffel and sports bags)

PAUL SMITH
108 Fifth Avenue
New York, NY 10011
212/627-9770
(Canvas and leather bags)

PAUL STUART
Madison Avenue at 45th
Street
New York, NY 10017
212/682-0320
(Travel accessories)

PRADA
45 East 57th Street
New York, NY 10022
212/308-2332

T. ANTHONY
445 Park Avenue
New York, NY 10022
212/750-9797
(Luggage and accessories)

TAKASHIMAYA
693 Fifth Avenue
New York, NY 10022
212/350-0100
(Luggage and accessories)

TERRA VERDE
120 Wooster Street
New York, NY 10012
212/925-4533
(Mesh bags and accessories)

TIFFANY & COMPANY
727 Fifth Avenue
New York, NY 10022
212/755-8000
(Travel accessories)

ZITOMER PHARMACY
969 Madison Avenue
New York, NY 10021
212/737-4480
(Travel-sized toiletries)

ZONA
97 Greene Street
New York, NY 10012
212/925-6750
(Handbags and luggage)

TEXAS

THE KING RANCH
SADDLE SHOP
201 East Kleberg Street
Kingsville, TX 78363
800/282-KING or
512/595-5761
*(Handcrafted luggage,
saddles, and hunting gear)*

WASHINGTON

JANSPORT
10411 Airport Road
Everett, WA 98204
800/426-9227 or
206/353-0200
(Outdoor gear)

NATIONAL AND INTERNATIONAL LISTINGS

AMERICAN TOURISTER
91 Main Street
Warren, RI 02885
401/245-2100 or
800/635-5505

BARNEYS NEW YORK
660 Madison Avenue
New York, NY 10022
212/826-8900 or
800/777-0087
(Travel cases and accessories)

BERGDORF GOODMAN
754 Fifth Avenue
New York, NY 10019
212/753-7300
(Leather goods and travel gear)

BLOOMINGDALE'S
1000 Third Avenue
New York, NY 10022
212/355-5900 for national
listings
(Luggage and travel gear)

BROOKS BROTHERS
346 Madison Avenue
New York, NY 10017
212/682-8800 or
800/274-1816 for catalogue
*(Luggage and travel
accessories)*

CHANEL
5 East 57th Street
New York, NY 10022
212/355-5050
(Handbags and luggage)

COACH
710 Madison Avenue
New York, NY 10021
212/319-1772 or
800/223-8647
(Luggage and accessories)

COLE HAAN
667 Madison Avenue
New York, NY 10021
212/421-8440
(Handbags)

CRATE & BARREL
646 North Michigan Avenue
Chicago, IL 60611
312/787-5900 or
800/323-5461 for nearest
location
*(Carry-on luggage and
travel gear)*

DILLARD'S
PARK PLAZA
Markam & University
Little Rock, AR 72205
501/661-0053
(Luggage and accessories)

EDDIE BAUER, INC.
600 Madison Avenue
New York, NY 10022
212/421-2450
(Outdoor wear and gear)

EMPORIO ARMANI
110 Fifth Avenue
New York, NY 10011
212/727-3240
(Bags and travel accessories)

EASTERN MOUNTAIN
SPORTS
1 Vose Farm Road
Peterborough, NH 03458
603/924-9571
(Backpacks, daypacks)

THE GAP
1 Harrison Street
San Francisco, CA 94105
415/777-0250
(Knapsacks and duffels)

HARTMANN LUGGAGE
1301 Hartmann Drive
Lebanon, TN 37087
800/331-0613

HENRI BENDEL
712 Fifth Avenue
New York, NY 10019
212/247-1100
(Handbags and accessories)

HOFFRITZ
331 Madison Avenue
New York, NY 10017
212/924-7300 for national
listings
(Travel accessories)

HOLD EVERYTHING
San Francisco Centre
855 Market Street, #208,
2nd Floor
San Francisco, CA 94103
415/546-0986
(Packing and travel gear)

MACY'S WEST
170 O'Farrell Street
San Francisco, CA 94102
415/393-3457 for
West Coast listings

NEIMAN MARCUS
1618 Main Street
Dallas, TX 75201
214/741-6911
(Handbags and accessories)

NORDSTROM
1501 Fifth Avenue
Seattle, WA 98101
206/628-2111 or
800/285-5800 for catalogue
(Luggage and accessories)

POLO/
RALPH LAUREN
867 Madison Avenue
New York, NY 10021
212/606-2100
(Luggage and handbags)

REI
1525 11th Avenue
Seattle, WA 98122
800/426-4840 for national
store listings
(Backpacks and duffels)

SAMSONITE
11200 East 45th Avenue
Denver, CO 80239
303/373-2000

SAKS FIFTH AVENUE
611 Fifth Avenue
New York, NY 10022
212/753-4000 for
U.S. listings

URBAN OUTFITTERS
1801 Walnut Street
Philadelphia, PA 19103
215/569-3131 or
215/564-2313 for U.S. listings
(Backpacks)

CATALOGUES AND MAIL ORDER

J. CREW
203 Front Street
New York, NY 10038
800/782-8244
(Day and overnight bags)

J. PETERMAN
COMPANY'S OWNER
MANUAL
13-18 Russell Cave Road
Lexington, KY 40505
606/268-2006 or
800/231-7341
(Day and overnight bags)

LAND'S END DIRECT
MERCHANTS
1 Land's End Lane
Dodgeville, WI 53595
800/356-4444
*(Luggage, attachés, and
purses)*

MUSEUM OF MODERN
ART DESIGN STORE
44 West 53rd Street
New York, NY 10019
212/ 767-1050 or
800/447-MOMA
(Handbags and accessories)

ORVIS
Historic Route 7A
Manchester, VT 05254
802/362-3622 or
800/541-3541
(Duffels and sporting gear)

REMO MAIL-ORDER
CATALOGUE
Oxford at Crown Street
Sydney, Australia
8/029-714
(Hip general store)

TILLEY ENDURABLES
300 Langer Road
West Seneca, NY 14224
800/338-2797 for catalogue
or listings
*(Travel clothes, including the
famous Tilley Hat)*

WATHNE
1095 Cranbury South River
Road, Suite 8
Jamesburg, NJ 08831
800/942-1166
(Duffels and sporting gear)

INTERNATIONAL LISTINGS

Australia

MELBOURNE

GEORGES
162 Collins Street
3/283-5555
(Upscale department store)

SYDNEY

DAVID JONES
P.O. Box 503
2/266-5544
(Upscale department store)

Canada

VANCOUVER

EDDIE BAUER
Pacific Centre
P.O. Box 10177
700 West Georgia Street
V7Y 1E4
604/683-4711

TORONTO

LOUIS VUITTON
110 Bloor Street West
M5S 2W7
416/968-3993

MONTREAL

JET-SETTER WEST
66 rue Laurier Ouest
H2T 2N4
514/271-5058
(Travel articles)

France

PARIS

HERMÈS
24, rue du Faubourg Saint-
Honoré
75008
40/17-47-17
(Leather bags and accessories)

LE MONDE SAUVAGE
82, rue Rambuteau
75008
40/26-28-33
(Luggage)

PRADA
5, rue de Grenelle
75006
45/48-53-14
(Luggage and accessories)

UPLA
22, rue de Grenelle
75007
40/26-49-96
*(Handbags inspired by
traditional hunting and
fishing bags)*

Germany

BERLIN

E. BRAUN & CO.
Kurfürstendamm 43
10719
30/881-3462
(Handbags and accessories)

MUNICH

LUDWIG BECK
Marienplatz 11
89/236-910
(Upscale department store)

MEY & EDLICH
Theatinerstrasse 7
89/290-0590
(Upscale department store)

Great Britain

LONDON

FORTNUM AND
MASON LTD.
181 Piccadilly
W1A 1ER
171/734-8040
(Hampers and luggage)

GUCCI
27 Old Bond Street
W1X 4HH
171/629-2716

HARVEY NICHOLS
109 Knightsbridge
SW1X 7RJ
171/235-5000

HERMÈS BOUTIQUE
179 Sloane Street
W1X 9QP
171/823-1014

LIBERTY
210-220 Regent Street
W1R 6AH
171/734-1234

LOEWE LEATHER
GOODS
130 New Bond Street
W1Y 9RA
171/493-3914

MARKS & SPENCER
PLC.
113 Kensington High Street
W8 5SQ
171/938-3711
(Department store)

MUJI
26 Great Marlborough
Street
W1V 1HL
171/494-1197
*(Generic lifestyle products
from Japan)*

MULBERRY
185 Brompton Road
Knightsbridge
SW1
171/225-0313
(Luggage and handbags)

PAUL SMITH
40-44 Floral Street
WC2 E9DG
171/379-7133
(Travel accessories)

SWAINE, ADENEY,
BRIGG & SONS LTD.
10 Old Bond Street
W1X 3DB
171/409-7277
(Luggage and travel goods)

W. & H. GIDDEN OF
LONDON, LTD.
15d Clifford Street
W1X 1RF
171/734-2788
(Saddlers since 1806)

Italy

MILAN

ETRO
Via Montenapoleone 3
2/55-02-01
(Leather goods)

PRADA
Galleria V. Emanuele 63-65
2/87-69-79
Via della Spiga 1
2/76-00-20-19
(Travel bags and accessories)

Japan

TOKYO

BE TRAVEL BY DESIGN
3-29-3 Jingu-mae, 2nd Floor
Shibuya-ku
3/3478-4230
(Luggage and travel gear)

LOFT
21-1 Udagawa
Shibuya-ku
3/3462-0111
(Trendy department store)

MUJI NO BRAND
GOODS
4-22-8 Taishidou
Setadayaku
3/3410-2323
(Generic lifestyle products)

TOKYU HANDS
12-18 Udagawa
Shibuya-ku
3/3476-5461
*(Department store; outdoor
gear)*

TRAVELLAND
Shinjuku Lumine #1 Bld. 5F
1-1-5 Nishi Shinjuku-ku
3/3348-5271
(Luggage and travel gear)

RESOURCES

CHIC SIMPLE STAFF

PARTNERS Kim & Jeff
ART DIRECTOR Wayne Wolf
ASSOCIATE ART DIRECTOR Alicia Yin Cheng
ASSOCIATE EDITOR Victoria C. Rowan
OFFICE MANAGER Joanne Harrison

ACKNOWLEDGMENTS

MANUFACTURER & RETAIL RESEARCH: Jeannette Durkan **LUGGAGE RESEARCH:** Jennifer Lisle **QUOTE RESEARCH:** Lige Rushing & Kate Doyle Hooper **ORIGINAL INTERVIEWS:** Cynthia Stuart **FASHION STYLISTS:** Amanda Manogue *(pages 62, 64, 65)* John Mather *(pages 66, 67, 68, 69)* **AND SPECIAL THANKS TO:** Connie Bang, Amy Capen, Tony Chirico, Jin Chung, M. Scott Cookson, Lauri Del Commune, Michael Drazen, Borden Elniff, Jane Friedman, Janice Goldklang, Meredith Harrington, Patrick Higgins, Katherine Hourigan, Dina Dell'Arciprete-Houser, Andy Hughes, Pamela Hunt, Carol Janeway, Barbara Jones-Diggs, Nicholas Latimer, William Loverd, Anne McCormick, Dwyer McIntosh, Sonny Mehta, Lan Nguyen, Ingrid Nystrom, Kumiko Ohta, Mitchell Rosenbaum, Janet Rouber, Ivor Spencer, Anne-Lise Spitzer, Meg Stebbins, Robin Swados, Takuyo Takahashi, Aileen Tse, Shelley Wanger.

COMMUNICATIONS

In your own well-packed travels if you see stores or products you feel are Chic Simple, let us know. We've gotten so many faxes, e-mails, and postcards about the other Chic Simple books we've created a catalog. If you would like to receive one FREE, send us some chocolate chip cookies along with your address to:

CHIC SIMPLE
84 WOOSTER STREET, NEW YORK, NY 10012
fax: (212) 343-9678
email address: **info@chicsimple.com**
compuserve number **72704,2346**
web site address: **http://www.chicsimple.com**

Stay in touch because "The more you know, the less you need."

TYPE

The text of this book was set in two typefaces: New Baskerville and Futura.

The ITC version of **NEW BASKERVILLE** is called Baskerville, which itself is a facsimile reproduction of types cast from molds made by John Baskerville (1706–1775) from his designs. Baskerville's original face was one of the forerunners of the type style known to printers as the "modern face"—a "modern" of the period A.D. 1800. **FUTURA** was produced in 1928 by Paul Renner (1878–1956), former director of the Munich School of Design, for the Bauer Type Foundry. Futura is simple in design and wonderfully restful in reading. It has been widely used in advertising because of its even, modern appearance in mass and its harmony with a great variety of other modern types.

SEPARATION AND FILM PREPARATION BY

APPLIED GRAPHICS TECHNOLOGIES
Carlstadt, New Jersey

PRINTED AND BOUND BY

BERTELSMANN PRINTING &
MANUFACTURING CORP.
Berryville, Virginia

HARDWARE

Power Macintosh 8100/80 and Quadra 700 personal computers; APS Technologies Syquest Drives; Radius Precision Color Display/20; Radius 24X series Video Board; Hewlett Packard LaserJet 4, Supra Fax Modem, Iomega Zip Drive.

SOFTWARE

QuarkXPress 3.3, Adobe Photoshop 2.5.1, Microsoft Word 6.0, FileMaker Pro 2.0, Adobe Illustrator 5.0.1.

MUSICWARE

Chris Isaak *(Heart-Shaped World)*, Assorted Artists *(Love Gets Strange—The Songs of John Hiatt)*, 10,000 Maniacs *(MTV Unplugged)*, Clint Black *(The Hard Way)*, Peggy Lee *(Collectors Series)*, Duran Duran *(The Tour Sampler)*, US3 *(Hand on the Torch)*, The Who *(Hooligans)*, Cocteau Twins *(Four-Calendar Café)*, the Breeders *(Last Splash)*, Bill Morrissey *(Night Train)*, Grand Funk Railroad *(Collectors Series)*, Tennessee Ernie Ford *(Collectors Series)*, Philip Glass *(Itaipu)*, Lil' Louis & the World *(journey with the lonely)*, Rozalla *(Everybody's Free)* Greg Brown *(Dream Cafe)*, Bird *(The Complete Charlie Parker on Verve)*

With special thanks to Cathy O'Brien of Capitol Records

"I have a simple philosophy.
Fill what's empty. Empty what's
full. Scratch where it itches."

ALICE ROOSEVELT LONGWORTH